Y0-BCW-200

Straight
from the
Heart
for GRADUATES

Straight From the Heart for Graduates

by

Richard Exley

Tulsa, Oklahoma

Straight From the Heart for Graduates
ISBN 1-56292-095-2
Copyright © 1995 by Richard Exley
P.O. Box 54744
Tulsa, Oklahoma 74155

Published by Honor Books
P.O. Box 55388
Tulsa, Oklahoma 74155

Presented to:

_____

On the Occasion of:

_____

Presented by:

_____

Date:

_____

DEDICATION

*To my brother Don who was
the first member of our family
to graduate from college.*

*And to my brother Bob who
earned his Ph.D. in spite of
nearly impossible odds.*

Thanks for showing us the way!

Contents

Make a Life, Not Just a Living

"*In your quest to build your career, to become financially secure, to be a success, you will be tempted to discard the simple things that give life its meaning.*"

Chapter 1

Make a Life, Not a Living

*C*ongratulations! You have completed your course of study and have been awarded your diploma, or degree, as the case may be. You may have graduated with honors, having been a serious student, but more likely your studies were not your highest priority. You had other concerns, things like your friends, your social life, athletics.

It may be years before you come to understand those of us who look back on our school years and bemoan the fact that we failed to apply ourselves. For now, you are just glad to be graduating.

The graduation ceremony is called commencement, for while you have completed your course of studies, this day also signals a beginning, a new start. As we were fond of saying in the sixties when I graduated, "Today is the first day of the rest of your life." That being the case, it is important to decide not just what you are going to do with the rest of your life, but how you are going to live it.

In his commencement address at the University of Northern Iowa on July 29, 1983, Robert James Waller, of *The Bridges of Madison County* fame, said: "Since I am dean of the School of Business, I am absolutely sure a number of you turned out expecting to get some hot tips on microcomputer stocks or the latest news on money supply fluctuations. Sorry. Nor am I going to lecture you on (1) how well educated you are, (2) what wonderful opportunities you have before you, or (3) the importance of making great and lasting changes out there.

"What I want to talk about is something a little different, something that makes all the living and doing you are so anxious to get on with worthwhile. More than that, it makes the living and doing better — better in terms of quality and quantity. I am going to talk about romance."[1]

Romance, according to Waller, is not so much about loving another person, but about loving life and living it to the very fullest. How different that is from the way most of us view life. For us it is a race to run, a mountain to climb, a challenge to meet or an obstacle to conquer. With grim determination we set out to do battle with the forces arrayed against us. Given that mindset, is it any wonder that while we may achieve success, we seldom experience fulfillment?

---

[1]Robert James Waller, *Old Songs in a New Cafe* (New York: Warner Books, Inc., 1994), p. 42.

Late in life one woman confessed, "First I was dying to finish high school and start college. And then I was dying to finish college and start working. And then I was dying to marry and have children. And then I was dying for my children to grow old enough for school so I could return to work. And then I was dying to retire. And now, I am dying...and suddenly I realize I forgot to live."[2]

Being young and idealistic, you may think it could never happen to you. The truth is, none of us expects to make the same mistakes as the generation that went before us, but unless we consciously choose a different route, we may well end up at the same place.

One of the great dangers we face is mistaking the accumulation of things for life.

"Since World War II, we have been in an era of frenzied consumerism. Consumption and accomplishment have been held up as the keys to happiness. We told ourselves that if we had the car, the house, the color TV, the right job, we'd made it. Our heroes became those people who had the most. Our values focused on things."[3]

---

[2]Anonymous, quoted in "Happiness Is..." by Barbara De Angelis, Ph.D. *Good Housekeeping*, October 1994, p. 77.

[3]Ibid.

Yet, things are just things, no matter how rare or expensive they may be. And poor indeed is the person who sacrifices his personhood in a mad quest to accumulate more and more things.

This tragic truth is graphically depicted in the story of the peasant shepherd. One day while grazing his sheep on a hillside he notices a wild-flower of unusual beauty. Turning aside to study it in more detail, he decides to pick it.

When he does, the whole hillside opens revealing a cave filled with chests of precious stones, as well as gold and silver coins. For a moment he stands transfixed, then he rushes into the cave and begins to fill his pockets. As he turns to go, heavy-laden with his new-found wealth, he hears a voice. It simply says, "Don't forget the best."

Quickly he empties his pockets and rummages through the chests of precious stones, searching for the "best" gem. To his untrained eye, they all appear about the same so once more he fills his pockets and pre-pares to leave. The voice speaks again, "Don't forget the best."

For the third time he makes a thorough search. Somewhere there must be a prize gem or a special piece of jewelry. No luck. Everything still looks the same to him. As he heads for the cave's entrance, his pockets filled to overflowing with precious stones, his fists bulging with gold and silver coins, the voice stops him in his tracks. "Don't forget the best." He has a troubling sense that he is somehow making a terrible mistake, but for the life of him, he can't imagine what it might be.

Ignoring the voice, he walks into the sunlight. As he does, the earth trembles, and he turns just in time to see the hillside closing. The last thing he sees is the beautiful wildflower, discarded in his mad scramble to gather all the wealth he could. At last he understands and, to his consternation, he discovers that without the wildflower all his new-found wealth has turned to dust.

As you embark on your career, your life, let the shepherd's experience serve as a warning. If you are not careful, the world's system will seduce you. In your quest to build your career, to become financially secure, to be a success, you will be tempted to discard the simple things that give life its meaning. But if you do, even your success will turn to dust.

Determine right now, on this "commencement" day, that *you are going to make a life and not just a living.* Choose to treasure the "best" no matter how hectic or demanding the world may become.

Take time to know God. Enjoy life's little pleasures — early morning prayer in a dim sanctuary, a good book, a few minutes alone at the end of a busy day. Treasure your relationships. Spend time with your family. Enjoy a good laugh at least once a day. Never be afraid to cry. Do this, and you will be a success whatever you achieve.

2

*Happiness Is a
Consequence,
Not a Goal*

"*Of* all the things you desire, happiness is probably the most elusive. It's like a butterfly — the harder you try to catch it, the more elusive it becomes."

Chapter 2

Happiness Is a Consequence, Not a Goal

Now that you have graduated, it is time to consider your future. What do you really want out of life? If you are like the majority of graduates, you want the American dream. You want financial security, meaningful work with an opportunity for advancement, your own home and a family, not to mention happiness.

Of all the things you desire, happiness is probably the most elusive. It's like a butterfly – the harder you try to catch it, the more elusive it becomes. But if you will be still, and wait patiently, it will light on your shoulder.

During his Hall of Fame career, Lou Brock became not only a clutch hitter and a fine defensive outfielder, but the greatest base stealer in the history of baseball, with 938 career steals. Hardly anyone who saw him early in his career, as a Chicago Cub, believed he was a future Hall of

Famer. After two full seasons in the major leagues, he was hitting only about .260 and was considered a defensive liability.

Ultimately, the Cubs gave up on him, and in 1964 he was traded to the Cardinals. Sportswriters and fans alike greeted his arrival in St. Louis with no little skepticism, but by the season's end Brock had proved his worth. Not only did he spark one of the greatest comebacks in National League history, as the Cardinals came from ten games back at the all-star break to win the pennant on the last day of the season, but he also played a key role as the Cardinals defeated the Yankees in the World Series.

Why, baseball buffs wonder, did Brock languish in Chicago, but blossom in St. Louis? There are probably several factors. Chicago was a power-hitting team, point out some, while St. Louis relied on speed, which was Brock's forte. Others have suggested it was just a matter of timing, that Brock was coming into his own when Chicago traded him.

Ernie Banks, a friend and a teammate of Brock's with the Cubs, thought he was trying too hard. According to Banks, Brock was driven to succeed, to excel; consequently, he was tying himself in knots.

Bob Kennedy, the Chicago manager, agreed. To prove his point, he once asked Brock to write his name on a piece of paper. Brock did it easily, without thinking. Then Kennedy asked him to write it again, slowly this time, thinking carefully about each letter. Brock complied and produced an entirely different signature, one so pinched and unrecognizable that no bank would have cashed a check with it.

"That," Kennedy told him, "is what you are doing at the plate."

When it comes to happiness, many of us are like Lou Brock – we try too hard. With single-minded determination we set out to be happy, and we are sure that given the right circumstances we will be. When we get the right job, when we can afford to drive the right car, when we get married, when we own our dream house, when we can take the vacation of a lifetime – then we will be happy. Unfortunately, life is filled with people whose experience proves otherwise. One by one they have achieved their goals only to discover that happiness still eludes them.

In truth, happiness is a consequence, not a goal. If you pursue it, you will never find it, but if you forget about being happy, and simply concentrate on living your life honorably, happiness will find you.

Will Durant is a case in point. He writes, "(For) many years I lost happiness. I sought it in knowledge, and found disillusionment. I sought it in writing, and found a weariness of the flesh. I sought it in travel, and my feet tired on the way. I sought it in wealth, and I found discord and worriment.

"And then one day, at a little station out on a wooded cliff near the sea, I saw a woman waiting in a tiny car, with a child asleep in her arms.

A man alighted from a train, walked to her quickly, embraced her, and kissed the child gently, careful lest he should awaken it. They drove off together to some modest home among the fields; and it seemed to me that happiness was with them.

"Today I have neglected my writing. The voice of a little girl calling to me, 'Come out and play,' drew me from my papers and my books. Was it not the final purpose of my toil that I should be free to frolic with her, and spend unharassed hours with the one who had given her to me? And so we walked and ran and laughed together, and fell in the tall grass, and hid among the trees; and I was young again.

"Now it is evening; while I write, I hear the child's breathing as she sleeps in her cozy bed. And I know that I have found what I sought. I perceive that if I will do as well as I can the tasks for which life has made me, I shall find fulfillment, and a quiet lane of happiness for many years."[1]

---

[1]Will Durant, quoted in *Dawnings: Finding God's Light in the Darkness*, edited by Phyllis Hobe (New York: Guideposts Associates, Inc., 1981) pp. 204,205.

CHAPTER

3

Attitude Is
Everything

" 'Two men looked out
from prison bars,
One saw the mud,
the other saw the
stars.' "

Chapter 3

Attitude Is Everything

During World War II, a young bride named Thelma Thompson went to live with her husband who was stationed at a U.S. Army training camp near the Mojave Desert, in California. From the first day she hated the place. She hated the dust, the loneliness, the tiny shack in which they had to live and most of all the unbearable heat – 125 degrees in the shade of a cactus. There was no one to talk to but Mexicans and Indians, and they couldn't speak English.

Finally, she became so utterly wretched, so full of self-pity, that she wrote her parents and told them she was coming home. Her father answered her letter with just two lines – two lines which Thelma says will always sing in her memory – which she says completely altered her life:

"Two men looked out from prison bars,

One saw the mud, the other saw the stars."

According to Thelma, she read those two lines over and over until she determined to find the good in her situation. She made up her mind to look for the stars.

Tentatively, she reached out to the natives, and to her surprise they received her overtures toward friendship warmly. When she showed interest in their weaving and pottery, they gave her presents of their favorite pieces, pieces which they refused to sell to the tourists.

She studied until she became an expert on the various forms of cactus and the yuccas and the Joshua trees. She learned about prairie dogs, watched for the desert sunsets and hunted for seashells that had been left there when the sands of the desert had been an ocean floor.

The Mojave Desert didn't change. The Indians didn't change. The wind still blew incessantly, the temperatures continued to reach 125 degrees, the tiny shack in which she lived with her husband was still claustrophobic, but none of that mattered anymore. Thelma was different.

By changing her attitude, she transformed a wretched experience into the most exciting adventure of her life. Instead of wallowing in self-pity, she wrote a book, a novel, about the desert, which was published under the title Bright Ramparts.[1] She looked out of her self-made prison and discovered the stars.

[1] C. Roy Angell, Baskets of Silver (Nashville: Broadman Press, 1955), pp. 102-104.

Hopefully, you will never find yourself stationed on the Mojave Desert, but you will undoubtedly face equally challenging circumstances. They may come in the form of a family tragedy, or a broken romance or a failed business venture. When they come, whatever form they take, you will find yourself faced with the same choice that confronted Thelma Thompson more than fifty years ago. You can succumb to your painful disappointments, or you can overcome them. You can see the mud, or the stars.

The choice is yours.

You cannot escape the tough times, they are inevitable. You can only prepare for them.

In order to maintain a positive attitude, I have found it helpful to believe the best, prepare for the worst and trust God with the rest.

Every situation we face affords a number of interpretations, all of which contain some element of truth. People with a positive attitude have developed the ability to focus on the possibilities rather than the problems. As a consequence, they often get things done when no one else can. For them, the world is filled with opportunities cleverly camouflaged as insurmountable obstacles.

Few things illustrate this point better than the story of the two shoe salesmen who were sent to an island to sell footwear. Upon discovering that everyone on the island went barefoot, one of the salesmen wired his home office and informed his supervisors that he was returning immediately. "No one wears shoes," he explained.

Confronted with the same facts, the second salesman reacted differently. He too wired the home office, but his telegram contained a different message: "Ship 10,000 pairs of shoes immediately. Everyone here needs them."

Don't misunderstand me. Maintaining a positive attitude doesn't mean that you become an unrealistic optimist. Even as you believe the best, you prepare for the worst. A positive attitude enables you to make the right decision, daring though it may be. And having made the right decision, you are then free to address the problems, both real and potential.

Years ago I developed a strategy that has served me well. I call it "Worst Case Scenario." Here's how it works. Once I have decided on a course of action, I try to imagine anything and everything that could possibly go wrong. After listing these gruesome possibilities, I formulate a plan of action for dealing with them should the need arise.

Of course, some of the possibilities are beyond my ability to countermand, which brings me to my third thought: Leave the rest to God.

Sooner or later you are going to face a situation which is simply beyond you. No matter how hard you try, you will not be able to turn things around. In that moment you will be tempted to despair.

Don't!

God has a long history of redeeming life's tragedies, of turning impossible situations into new beginnings. As Saint Paul says, "...we know that in all things God works for the good of those who love him, who have been called according to his purpose."[2]

---

[2]Romans 8:28.

CHAPTER

4

Don't Be Afraid
To Fail

" '...go ahead and make mistakes. Make all you can. Because, remember, that's where you'll find success. On the far side of failure.' "

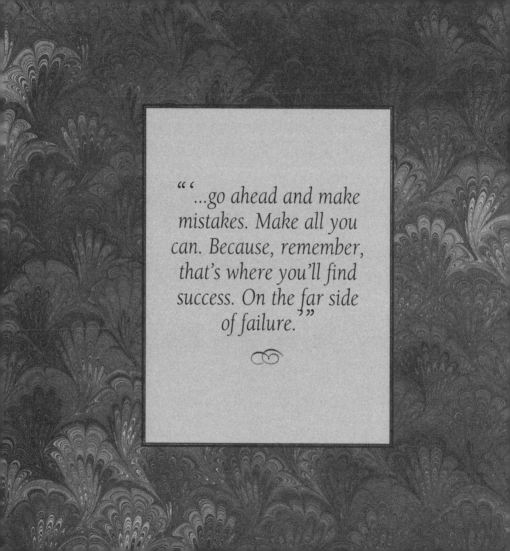

Chapter 4

Don't Be Afraid To Fail

When we see successful people, we often assume that they "got all the breaks," that they were always in the right place at the right time, that they've never failed, never been rejected. If the truth were known, very few people accomplish anything worthwhile the first time they attempt it. In fact, even the most successful people generally have a checkerboard career of both success and failure.[1]

"When Nathaniel Hawthorne lost his position in the Custom House at Salem, Massachusetts, he came home utterly defeated to tell his wife that he was a complete failure. To his amazement she greeted his dismal news with delight, saying, 'Now you can write your book.' So he sat down and wrote *The Scarlet Letter*, still considered by many critics as the greatest novel ever written in our country."[2]

---

[1]Richard Exley, *Blue-Collar Christianity* (Tulsa: Honor Books, 1989), p. 67.

[2]Ilion T. Jones, *God's Everlasting Yes* (Waco: Word Books, 1969), p. 24.

"Philip Brooks, the noted Episcopal minister who died in the 1890's, had planned to be a teacher and had prepared himself for the profession of teaching. But he failed so ingloriously that he became despondent. Then he prepared himself for the ministry. In this calling he made a huge success."[3]

For years Alexander Graham Bell was a failure, at least he suffered one humiliating setback after another. He spent much of his life being laughed at and ridiculed as he crisscrossed New England trying to raise venture capital for the production of his invention – the telephone. Today nobody laughs at Bell. But he had to overcome failure in order to succeed.

When Walt Disney went around Hollywood with his little "Steamboat Willie" cartoon idea, he was bankrupt and by all normal standards a failure.

Johnny Carson's first effort at his own network show was a terrible flop and for years he was a forgotten man. Today he is the standard by which all TV personalities are judged.[4]

Like many others, all these people experienced painful, and sometimes humiliating, failure, but they refused to give up. Instead of allowing

---

[3]Ibid.

[4]Exley, pp. 67,68.

failure to defeat them, they stubbornly pursued their dreams and eventually attained them.

When Arthur Gordon was still an unpublished writer trying to launch his career, he was privileged to have lunch with Thomas J. Watson, President of International Business Machines. At some point during lunch Mr. Watson offered him a job with IBM and Gordon turned it down, explaining that he aspired to be a writer. Once he had shared his dream, he poured out the painful details of his writing failures and the endless rejection slips.

Leaning back in his chair, Mr. Watson said, "You're making a common mistake. You're thinking of failure as the enemy of success. But it isn't that at all. Failure is a teacher – a harsh one, perhaps, but the best. You say you have a desk full of rejected manuscripts? That's great! Every one of those manuscripts was rejected for a reason. Have you pulled them to pieces looking for that reason? That's what I have to do when an idea backfires or a sales program fails. You've got to put failure to work for you.

"You can be discouraged by failure – or you can learn from it. So go ahead and make mistakes. Make all you can. Because, remember, that's where you'll find success. On the far side of failure."[5]

---

[5]Arthur Gordon, *A Touch of Wonder* (Old Tappan: Fleming H. Revell Company, 1974), p. 73.

Apparently Mr. Gordon took his advice to heart because he became a highly successful author. Two of his books were made into movies, and his articles have appeared in prominent magazines including *Reader's Digest* and *Guideposts*.

What am I trying to say? Just this: failure isn't final. In fact, many of history's greatest leaders were considered abysmal failures by their contemporaries before they finally ascended to power. The two most notable being Abraham Lincoln and Winston Churchill. Both men came to power in a crisis hour of their nation's history following a string of ignominious failures. And each in his own way became the greatest leader his nation has ever known. As Lincoln lay dying in a little rooming house across from Ford's Theatre where he was shot, a former detractor (Edwin Stanton) said, "There lies the most perfect ruler of men the world has ever seen...[and] now he belongs to the ages."[6]

It is not failure that makes or breaks a person, but how he responds to it. If you can learn from your failures, if you can persist in spite of failure, if you can maintain a positive attitude, a forward look, then you will succeed in life no matter how many times you may fail.

---

[6]Charles R. Swindoll, *Growing Strong in the Seasons of Life* (Portland: Multnomah Press, 1983), p. 69.

"So go ahead and make mistakes. Make all you can. Because, remember, that's where you'll find success. On the far side of failure."[7]

---
[7]Gordon, p. 73.

CHAPTER

5

The Measure of Success

" *The* rampant con-
sumerism of our age
is unparalleled in the
history of mankind. It
will tempt you to believe
that your value as a
person is determined by
the things you possess."

⧂

Chapter 5

The Measure of Success

"*I* was just a teenager," she says, speaking with a heavy accent, "when the Russian army arrived in our village near the end of World War II. The first thing they did was order everyone to meet in the plaza – the town square."

Her name is Sigi, and she is an East German refugee. As she speaks, in a voice we have to strain to hear, a somber silence settles over the room. Her words paint a picture, and I can see it all – the frightened families huddling together against the cold, Russian tanks in the background, bombed-out buildings.

Hard-eyed Russian soldiers stand guard as an officer mounts the steps and begins to speak. "At sunrise you will gather here and be marched to a detention camp to await relocation. You will only be allowed to take what you can carry. Choose carefully. If you lag behind, you will be shot."

Before daylight, Sigi and her family make their way to the plaza where a crowd has already gathered. Occasionally someone speaks, but for the most part the square is unnaturally quiet. It is cold, and their breath hangs in the semi-darkness like a warm vapor. Glancing around, Sigi observes that her family is not the only ones who have brought far more than they can hope to carry. All around her, young and old alike, stagger beneath the burden of the things they simply cannot live without.

In the distance she hears the roar of engines, and then headlights pierce the waning darkness as a troop truck turns the corner and slows to a stop. Soldiers pour out of the rear of the truck and began shoving the town's people into a ragged column. The command is given to move out, and the march is underway. They haven't gone more than a mile before an old man stumbles and falls. Without giving him a chance to get up, a soldier shoots him.

"Let that be a warning to you," he snarls to the rest of the group.

It is still early, the sun has hardly cleared the trees on the eastern horizon, but already the refugees are discarding their prize possessions. Soon the roadside is littered with silverware, antique clocks and family heirlooms. It's terribly sad, and several of the women weep as they are forced to abandon things that have been in their family for generations.

Here is where Sigi's story takes its most tragic turn. "Scores of people," she tells us, "some of them close friends, simply cannot part with their possessions. Rather than discard a single thing, they lag behind and are shot down mercilessly."

"That's the danger of materialism," she says, with a conviction that leaves no room for debate. "You start out owning things, and they end up owning you! Sometimes it gets so bad that you can't give up a single possession, not even to save your soul."

Opening her Bible she reads, "Then he [Jesus] said to them, 'Watch out! Be on your guard against all kinds of greed; a man's life does not consist in the abundance of his possessions.'"[1]

The luncheon ends on this sober note, and we file out, hardly speaking, each of us absorbed in his own thoughts.

More than twenty years have passed since I heard Sigi speak, but I have never forgotten her words. They are, I believe, more relevant today than they were the day she first spoke them. I only wish that I could help you to sense something of the urgency she made me feel.

Without a doubt, materialism is one of the most challenging temptations you will face as you enter adulthood.

---

[1] Luke 12:15.

The rampant consumerism of our age is unparalleled in the history of mankind. It will tempt you to believe that your value as a person is determined by the things you possess. The latest verse of this age-old song goes something like this: If you live in the right neighborhood, drive the right automobile, have the latest electronic gadgets and dress in designer clothes, then you are someone of significance.

The fallacy of such thinking should be readily obvious, but often it is not. Too soon you may find yourself buying things you don't need and can't afford in order to impress people you don't even like. As a consequence, credit card debt and financial woes mount, but they are just the tip of the iceberg. The real problem goes deeper, much deeper. You thought you were buying things to own only to discover, as Sigi says, that those very things now own you!

I am often asked how a person can guard his heart against materialism. It isn't easy, believe you me. The world's system is always encroaching, always tempting us to adopt its value system, but if we are serious we can overcome.

After several less than successful strategies I finally hit on one that works for me. In order to guard my heart against materialism, I must constantly remind myself that I am only a steward. Nothing I possess is really mine. Everything I have belongs to God. He has simply entrusted these things to my care, and one day I will give an account of how I managed them.

With that thought in mind, I have deliberately chosen to live beneath my means in order to invest more in the Kingdom of God. It's the only way I know that a person can keep materialism from overrunning his heart.

CHAPTER

6

Discovering Your Destiny

*"...God has a plan
for your life, and He
wants to make it
known to you."*

Chapter 6

Discovering Your Destiny

As unbelievable as it may seem, God has a plan for your life. He cares about your education, your career and the person you marry. In fact, the Bible says His plan for you was written in detail even before you were born.[1]

Some people find that intimidating. They don't want anyone, not even God, telling them how to live their life. God's will, according to their way of thinking, is arbitrary and inhibiting.

Nothing could be further from the truth. God's will for your life is custom designed with you in mind. Taking your talents, your personality and your background into consideration, God formulates a plan that will enable you to maximize your abilities while experiencing genuine fulfillment.

---

[1]See Psalm 139:13-16.

For the most part, the frustrations people experience come, not from doing the will of God, but from trying to avoid it.

Better than anyone else, including you, God knows what will fulfil you, and with that in mind He designs a plan for your life.

The first step in discovering God's plan for you is unconditional surrender. Many of us pray, "Lord, show me Your will," so we can decide whether we want to do it or not. But God doesn't make His will known simply to satisfy our curiosity. It is revealed most frequently as marching orders to the committed, to the one who has prayed, "I'll go where You want me to go, I'll do what You want me to do."

"There are four ways in which He reveals His will to us," according to Hannah Whitall Smith, " – through the Scriptures, through providential circumstances, through the convictions of our own higher judgment, and through the inward impressions of the Holy Spirit on our minds."[2]

While God has used all four of these methods to communicate His will to me on one occasion or another, He usually speaks to me through the inward impressions of the Holy Spirit. Most often I have a sense when something is right, when it's God's will. It's a "gut feeling," and over the years I have learned to trust it.

---

[2]Hannah Whitall Smith, *The Christian's Secret of a Happy Life* (Westwood: Fleming H. Revell Company, 1952), p. 93.

Inevitably, someone wants me to be more specific. "What exactly," they ask, "do you mean by a 'gut feeling?'" When pressed, I define it as my surrendered desires.

Here's how it works.

I bring all of my hopes and dreams, all of my ambitions and desires, and lay them at the foot of the Cross. I give them to God, praying, "Lord, I give You permission to change my desires, to superimpose Your will on mine. Now guide me through my desires." Then I do what I want to do, believing that my desires now reflect God's direction for my life.

Based on my own experience, I agree with Hannah Whitall Smith when she says, "...His suggestions will come to us, not so much as commands from the outside as desires springing up within. They will originate in our will; we shall feel as though we *desired* to do so and so, not as though we *must*."[3]

While I trust these inner promptings, I do not accept them as infallible. In fact, I submit them to three tests. First, the Word test: Is this desire scriptural? Second, the time test: Now that I've waited a while, has the intensity of my desire grown or waned? And third, the door test: Has God opened a door of opportunity so I can pursue my desire?

---

[3]*Ibid.*, p. 100.

Let's consider these one at a time.

First, the Word test. I ask myself: What do the Scriptures say about this desire? Is it prohibited by direct command or scriptural principle? Remember, God's special guidance will never violate His revealed will, which is expressed in the Word.

The late A. W. Tozer used to say that we should never seek guidance about what God has already forbidden. Nor should we ever seek guidance in the areas where God has already said yes and given us a command. In those instances, what we need is not guidance, but obedience.

If my desire passes the Word test, then I submit it to the time test. If a desire is really divine direction, then the longer I delay, the stronger it becomes. As Jeremiah said, "'...his word is in my heart like fire, a fire shut up in my bones....'"[4]

On the other hand, if it is just a personal whim and I wait, surrendered, submitting it to the time test, it will fade away.

According to David Wilkerson, "The will of God grows on you. That which is of God will fasten itself on you and overpower and possess your entire being. That which is not of God will die – you will lose interest.

---

[4]Jeremiah 20:9.

But the plan of God will never die. The thing God wants you to do will become stronger each day in your thoughts, in your prayers, in your planning. It grows and grows!"[5]

Finally, if it's compatible with the Word, and if it passes the time test, then I submit it to the door test. Keith Miller says, "This is sort of like rattling door handles to see if you can find a door which is unlocked...."[6]

More than twelve years ago I had an experience that illustrates this principle perfectly. For almost five and a half years I had served as pastor of the Church of the Comforter in Craig, Colorado. They were some of the best years of my life. While there, I wrote two books, built a new house and led the church through a successful building program. Yet, after five years I was feeling restless. The new facilities were finished, and the congregation seemed ready to launch new ministries into the community, but my heart wasn't in it.

After the restlessness had persisted for several weeks, I prayed: "God, I don't trust my emotions. I feel like it is time for me to make a move, yet I can't be sure. If this restlessness comes from You, if it's time for me to change churches, then You will have to open the door."

---

[5]David Wilkerson, *I'm Not Mad at God* (Minneapolis: Bethany Fellowship, Inc., 1967), p. 32.
[6]Keith Miller and Bruce Larson, *The Edge of Adventure* (Waco: Word Books Publisher, 1974), p. 214.

Within two weeks I received a telephone call from Christian Chapel in Tulsa, Oklahoma. In my fifteen years of ministry I had never preached in Oklahoma, and no one in Tulsa had ever heard of Richard Exley. Still, through a series of divinely directed events, I came to the attention of the pulpit committee, and they invited me to interview for the position of senior pastor.

When the congregation extended the call, my wife and I accepted and moved to Tulsa. Things weren't easy; they seldom are. Our house in Colorado didn't sell for a year, Brenda was forced to work outside the home in order to make ends meet and our daughter Leah had trouble adjusting to her new school; yet in it all we had a sense of security. Beneath all the surface storms, we had an underlying calm – the confidence that comes from being obedient, from being in the center of God's perfect will.

Now, fourteen years later, I am more convinced than ever that it was God's guidance that brought us to Christian Chapel. It began with a restlessness that wouldn't go away; then God sovereignly opened the door, and the rest, as they say, is history.

Remember, God has a plan for your life, and He wants to make it known to you. There are risks, to be sure. You may misunderstand and do the wrong thing, but He is able to take even your unintentional mistakes and make them contribute to your ultimate growth. "The Lord will fulfill his purpose for (you)...."[7]

If you wait until you have resolved every doubt, every question, before following God, you will never do anything with your life. You must step out by faith; you must go and do whatever it is you think God is directing you to do. Being assured, as Paul Tournier says, that, "God guides us, despite our uncertainties and our vagueness, even through our failings and mistakes."[8]

It helps me to think of guidance as a miner's cap with its built-in lamp whose feeble beam penetrates the darkness only a step or two. As the miner steps out, the light penetrates ever deeper, one step at a time. So it is with God's guidance. We receive further direction only as we walk in the light He has already given us.

[7]Psalm 138:8.

[8]Paul Tournier, *Reflections on Life's Most Crucial Questions* (New York: Harper and Row, Publishers, 1976), p. 123.

C H A P T E R

7

*The Friendship
Factor*

"*In truth, few things in life are more important than the choice of your friends. They will influence your values, help you shape your character and determine to no little degree what you make of yourself.*"

Chapter 7

The Friendship Factor

*F*or all he achieved as a major league baseball player, Mickey Mantle never fully lived up to his potential. When Mantle was a rookie, legendary New York Yankees manager Casey Stengel said, "This guy's going to be better than Joe DiMaggio and Babe Ruth."[1] By Mantle's own admission, it didn't happen.

The reasons are probably numerous, but to my way of thinking one of the significant factors was Mantle's choice of friends. When he joined the Yankees as a nineteen-year-old rookie in 1951, he became fast friends with Billy Martin and Whitey Ford, two of the hardest drinking players on the team. Prior to this time, Mantle hardly ever had a drink, but soon he was participating in marathon drinking bouts with Billy Martin to see who could drink the other under the table.

---

[1]Mickey Mantle with Jill Lieber, "My Time in a Bottle," Reader's Digest, December 1994, p. 90.

"After games on the road," he admits, "my teammates Billy Martin and Whitey Ford and I were wild men. We drank up a storm."[2]

While acknowledging that injuries shortened his career, Mantle says, "Truth is, after a knee operation, I'd be out drinking instead of doing rehab. God gave me a great body to play with, and I didn't take care of it."[3]

Mantle has never blamed anyone but himself for his drinking problems. Still, I cannot help but wonder what his career, and his life for that matter, might have been like if he had chosen his friends more wisely. Perhaps things would have turned out differently had he become friends with someone like Yankee teammate Bobby Richardson who was a family man and a teetotaler.

In truth, few things in life are more important than the choice of your friends. They will influence your values, help shape your character and determine to no little degree what you make of yourself. Choose them wisely, and they will prove an invaluable asset. By the same token, the wrong friends can cause you more grief than you can imagine.

When I use the term friends, I am not talking about people with whom you have only a casual relationship, or a business relationship.

[2]Ibid., p. 89.

[3]Ibid., p. 90.

They may be friends in the broadest sense, but they are not "Jonathan and David" type friends. While you should be friendly with and interested in everyone with whom you associate, you should only open your heart and life to those true friends who bring out the best in you, and vice versa.

How, you may be wondering, should you go about choosing your friends, what criteria should you use? Above all else, be cautious. Don't rush things, no matter how interesting or exciting your potential friend may seem. Time has a way of providing situations that reveal character defects that are not always readily obvious. Many hurtful experiences can be avoided simply by taking things more slowly. Even a good friendship can be enhanced when it is constructed patiently, little by little.

I have heard these real friends called "five-finger friends" – those you can count on the fingers of one hand. They are the kind of friends who are there for you no matter what happens. And it goes without saying that you are there for them as well. Many a person has been sustained in the hour of personal tragedy by such a friend, and across the course of a lifetime such close relationships will prove absolutely priceless.

In building this kind of friendship, it is important that you share the same faith – the same core beliefs about Jesus Christ, sin, salvation and eternal life. You can only provide each other the life-sustaining support required of this type of relationship if you have the same fundamental beliefs.

A crisis is simply no time to be debating the goodness of God or the power of prayer. In that difficult hour, we all need someone who will strengthen our own wavering faith, someone who will let us lean on them.

Five-finger friends are also invaluable because they hold us accountable. Well do I remember a time when I was considering entering into a business agreement with a group that was involved in an enterprise which violated my ethical standards. I rationalized that our venture was a totally separate entity (which it was), but when I thought of sharing the details with my five-finger friends I found myself hedging. Finally, I concluded that if I couldn't share all the details with them – because they might not "understand" – then I shouldn't become involved. Thankfully, I did not, and only God knows what potential embarrassment I was spared because of our friendship.

While a shared faith is the first criterion for a five-finger friendship, it is not the last. All of us know of people who profess the same beliefs that we do, yet whose lives are filled with inconsistencies. Given this sobering fact, we must develop a more detailed criterion. Thankfully, Solomon has already done that for us. Consider these thoughts from one of the wisest of all men.

"A gossip betrays a confidence; so avoid a man who talks too much."[4]

---

[4]Proverbs 20:19.

"Do not make friends with a hot-tempered man, do not associate with one easily angered, or you may learn his ways and get yourself ensnared."[5]

"Do not join those who drink too much wine or gorge themselves on meat, for drunkards and gluttons become poor, and drowsiness clothes them in rags."[6]

"Like a bad tooth or a lame foot is reliance on the unfaithful in times of trouble."[7]

Did you get that? A five-finger friend should not talk too much or be hot-tempered, nor should he be a heavy drinker. And perhaps most important of all, he should be trustworthy, someone who has proved his faithfulness in time of trouble.

By the same token, Solomon also provides some positive characteristics for which to look. For instance he says, "He who walks with the wise grows wise...."[8] And, "...the pleasantness of one's friend springs from his earnest counsel."[9] Finally, "A man of knowledge uses words with restraint, and a man of understanding is even-tempered."[10]

---

[5]Proverbs 22:24,25.
[6]Proverbs 23:20,21.
[7]Proverbs 25:19.
[8]Proverbs 13:20.
[9]Proverbs 27:9.
[10]Proverbs 17:27.

One final thought. I concur with Jerry Jenkins who counseled his son: "I urge you to limit your five-finger friends to your same sex, no matter how someone else might click with you or how you resonate with an individual."[11]

The physical attraction between men and women who form a strong emotional bond is simply too great to risk. Even if you never do anything physically inappropriate, the kind of emotional bond which you share should be reserved for you and your spouse. The quality of your marriage depends on it.

In order to build the kind of friendships we have been talking about, it is necessary to become that kind of person, that kind of friend. In a moment of loneliness you may be tempted to pray, "Lord, give me a friend like that." Instead I urge you to pray, "Lord, make me a friend like that."

---

[11]Jerry B. Jenkins, As You Leave Home (Colorado Springs: Focus on the Family Publishing, 1993), p. 115.

CHAPTER

8

*Finding the Love
of Your Life*

"How, you may be wondering, will you know who is right for you? It's not nearly as difficult as you might imagine, but it does require clear-eyed objectivity and good judgment."

∞

Chapter 8

Finding the Love of Your Life

*F*ew things in life will affect your future happiness and well-being more than your choice of a mate. Marry the right person, and marriage will be an ongoing source of joy and encouragement. Marry the wrong person, and you are likely to experience more pain and anger than you ever thought possible.

How, you may be wondering, will you know who is right for you? It's not nearly as difficult as you might imagine, but it does require clear-eyed objectivity and good judgment.

Since everyone knows that it is virtually impossible to be objective once having fallen in love, it is critically important to set high standards in courtship. No one can go far wrong by dating only those persons who qualify as potential candidates for marriage. Those who ignore this general rule leave themselves open to all kinds of messy situations.

I am reminded of a young man who sought my counsel some years ago. He was engaged to be married, and as the wedding approached he was assailed with misgivings.

"Please pray," he asked, "that God will reveal His will regarding my wedding."

Before praying, I asked him a few questions, and to my surprise I learned that his fiancee was not a believer. Confronted with this information, I kindly told him I could pray, but that there was really no need. God's will in regard to this matter was already on record. Opening my Bible, I read, "Do not be yoked together with unbelievers. For what do righteousness and wickedness have in common? Or what fellowship can light have with darkness?....What does a believer have in common with an unbeliever?"[1]

At this point he was faced with an "impossible decision." On the one hand he wanted to be obedient to the Scriptures, but on the other hand he was so emotionally entangled with his fiancee that he couldn't imagine breaking their engagement. Leaving my office he was visibly torn.

Watching him walk away, I could not help thinking that he could have spared himself this heart-rending dilemma if only he had refused to date anyone who did not share his faith.

---

[1] 2 Corinthians 6:14,15.

You may think that is a little extreme; after all, you are not even thinking of marriage yet. Besides, you know of at least one situation, maybe two, where marriage to an unbeliever led to his or her conversion.

I grant you all of that, but for every "exception" I can point to a long line of tragedies. In the best cases, such marriage "partners" simply live in two different worlds. Though they may have several things in common, on this most critical issue they are worlds apart. In most instances, things are not nearly so congenial. Religion is a source of constant contention, and their marriage suffers for it. Usually, the believing spouse forsakes the practice of his/her faith in order to effect some kind of peace in the home. Not infrequently, such marriages end in divorce.

In addition to sharing the same faith and commitment to the Lord Jesus Christ, there are other factors to be considered. "Christians, like nonbelievers, are unique and it does not follow that a marriage will be successful and stable simply because both people are followers of Jesus Christ. Marriage selection is best when the man and woman are similar in such variables as age, interests, values, socioeconomic level and education."[2]

In selecting a mate, you should also look for complimentary needs. "If both people enjoy social contacts but one person is outgoing and the

---

[2]Gary R. Collins, Ph.D., *Christian Counseling* (Waco: Word Books Publisher, 1980), p. 148.

other a little shy, this can be complimentary. If, in contrast, one person loves parties and the other is a recluse, these contradictory needs make conflict almost inevitable."[3]

Complimentary needs strengthen a marriage, while contradictory needs require frequent resolution and place enormous strain on the relationship.

You may be thinking: If the only people I date are those who meet these standards, how will I know who is the "right one" for me? The determining factor is emotional resonance – that indescribable feeling of being in love. You will just know. It will feel "right." The "spark" will be there.

Notice that I mention emotional resonance last. It should not even enter your thinking unless your potential mate shares your Christian convictions, comes from a similar background and has complimentary needs. Then, and only then, should you consider emotional resonance.

Far too many couples begin and end here. They never consider anything else. Obviously that is unwise, but it would be equally unwise to ignore such feelings or to overlook the lack of them.

What about the will of God? you may be asking. Doesn't He have anything to say about the person I marry?

---

[3]Ibid.

Good question. Of course, God cares who you marry, and you should always seek His guidance. Be assured though that His personal guidance will never contradict His will as it is revealed in the Scriptures. As a general rule, it will not violate reason either.

Better than anyone else, God knows that marital compatibility is dependent, to a significant degree, on the criteria we have considered. Therefore, it is unlikely that He will lead you to marry a person with whom you are obviously incompatible. He may, however, direct you not to marry a person who seems perfect for you. If that happens, yield to His guidance. God knows what He is doing, and you can be assured that He has your best interests at heart.

Let me conclude with two final thoughts. First, be careful not to confuse marriage with ministry.

Marriage is a partnership, a bonding, where the partners share equally in giving and receiving love. It requires two emotionally whole people to make it work.

Ministry, on the other hand, involves a primary giver and a primary recipient. It may be rewarding for the one doing the ministry, but it is not renewing. It is draining, especially when continued over an extended period.

A marriage based on this ministry model is doomed to mediocrity at best and possibly failure. Ask yourself: Is my potential spouse emotionally whole? Does he/she give as much as he/she takes?

If the answer to these questions is no, then beware!

One last consideration. Ask yourself: Am I prepared for marriage?

It is not only important to marry the right person, it is equally important to be the right person. Begin now to develop and refine your marriageability traits. The success of your marriage and your future happiness depends on it.

Other books by Richard Exley
are available at your local bookstore.

To contact the author, write:

Richard Exley
P.O. Box 54744
Tulsa, Oklahoma 74155

*Please include your prayer requests
when you write.*

Tulsa, Oklahoma